Things you and
I can relate to

Things you and
I can relate to

Jerome Miller

To order additional copies of this book, contact:
Xlibris
844-714-8691
www.Xlibris.com
Orders@Xlibris.com
817685

Acknowledgment

FIRST THING FIRST

All the honor, praise, and glory be to *God*. For he is head of my life, and through his grace, this book was completed. I would like to thank my family, teachers, and friends for their motivation, inspiration, and support. I furthermore would like to give a special thanks to my wife and my daughter for their listening ear to hear these poems read over and over.

CREDITS

Senior Partner...................................GOD
Senior Editor....................................GOD
Senior Emotion Consultant.................GOD
Head Writer......................................GOD
His Assistant....................................Me

Introduction

Within the pages of this book are words of wisdom, spiritual and inspirational.

Some of these words are from the old school, and some of them are from the new. But some are just imagined so that you and I can relate to.

This book is meant to bring out some of those memories that are locked up inside of you.

Remember, these are those memories, the ones that you and I can relate to.

I hope this book will inspire you and serve as food for thought. I hope that you can say that some of the things that are in this book are the ones that you and I can relate to.

The Best Man He Can Be

Jerome was born and raised in Cincinnati, Ohio. He is somebody's husband, father, son, brother, cousin, and friend. He was built to be the best man he can be. While as a child, he played, he lied, he cheated, and he cried. He did all these things under his family's watchful eyes. He was blessed to have good role model that taught him the very best. They kept him focused and gave him hopes and dreams. They taught him all these things and showed him what they mean. One day Jerome got into a fight, but he didn't know how. Jerome's brother step in and won that fight; he made Jerome very proud. His family always made him feel important and free; that's why Jerome acts the way that he acts; that's just him. So to Jerome's family, his wife, daughter, parents, aunts, uncles, brother, sisters, cousins, teachers, and friends, all can see that they all made him . . .

the best man he can be.

Life and You

In life, it's not important what job you do; it's more important, while at your lowest, what other people will do for you. Life can be cruel, kind, or sweet; it can have you being born in a rich and wealthy family or in a poor one, with no bed for you to sleep. Life isn't easy, but it's sure not hard. If you give life half a chance, life can give you a brand new start. Skin color, age, fortune, or fame, about these things, life doesn't care. Then there will be times you may think that life is playing a trick on you and has given you a double dare. Life can bring you joy. Life can bring you pain. Life can make you wish for sunshine. Life can make you pray for rain. In life, it may not be your turn to get put to the test. Your turn might be bigger; your turn might be next. If, in life, your good outweighs your bad, then don't complain. You can't always have sunshine; sometimes it has to rain. If you make the best of life and don't let life make you, if you live life to the fullest, life will live inside of you. And when life is through with you and your turn is next, you can't let someone cut in front of you; it's your turn, and you will be next. So take control of your life so you can be you. Remember, no one else can live your life; you have to live for you.

Contents

A Birthday Card—Love 1

A Child 2

A Friend 64

A Greeter 40

A Lie 15

A New Beginning 3

Angels 8

A Note from Momma 28

A Play Place for Me to Roam 59

Are You a Giver or Taker? 29

A Strong Gentleman 4

A Wish in a Prayer 6

Beauty Is More Than Skin Deep 9

Do You Have the Time? 5

Fast to Slow 30

Flowers 10

Food 42

Funeral 48

Good Morning 12

Happy Days Are Here Again 13

He, We, and I 65

I Can Only Imagine 14

If I Could Paint 32

I Wonder 15

JCU—All of Us 16

Just in Time 17

Listen—Memories 18

Marbles—Kick 'Em— Math 19

Mothers 44

My Biological Clock 47

My Dear Friend 46

My Father, My Hero 20

My Father's Son 34

Our Family 35

Our Holiday—A Delivery Man 21

People 23

People and Material Things...22

Phyllis...49

Seventeen at War...36

Sisters/Sisters-in-Law 24

Small Towns 52

Smile 51

That Feeling 54

The Title of a Man 56

The Weather...57

The World Is a Great Place...58

The World Lives On...25

Today 14

Veterans and Retirees Salute..26

We've Won 60

What Room Is It? 38

What Will You Say? 39

What Would You Do?...61

Who Will Come to Visit Me? 62

Would you? I would. 31

Your Heart and Head 43

A Birthday Card

To you, on your birthday, a card I never gave,
but I thank the Lord for your life
in my lifetime that he made.
So now, at this time,
I can say
that to you, for your birthday,
a card I still never gave.
Happy birthday to you.

Love

For whom my heart beats for.
That which pumps the blood through my veins,
And as we kiss and crest.
You and I, my wife,
We call it love.

A Child

Imagine, for a moment, this world without a child.
There would be no one to play with puppies
and no one to share a smile.
A child has an endless task sent from up above,
sent with a pocket full of candy,
sent with a heart full of love.
A child will always smile when they play with one another.
A child will always frown when it's time the take a bath
or when they can't find their mom or dad.
Just as you get close to your child,
It's time for them to go.
As you watch your child grow,
there are a few things you will come know.
When a child comes to you with that gleam in their eyes,
you will know that they have found that special someone,
and it's time for them to go.
Goodbye, Mom and Dad.

A New Beginning

How often we wish to have a new beginning;
a chance to wipeout our mistakes,
a chance to turn our failures into winnings.
It doesn't take a year or two
to have a brand new start.
It only takes a deep desire,
like the one that's in your heart.
So never give up in despair
and think that you are through.
For there is always a tomorrow
and a chance to start out brand new.
Start now,
and a new beginning
will be waiting on you.

A Strong Gentleman

It's not my age that makes me somebody.
It's not my height that makes me grown.
Don't take my kindness as my weakness,
and don't think my color makes me ashamed.
God made me this color,
and my parents gave me a name.
I am a strong but humble gentleman.

Do You Have the Time?

Do you have the time?
We all have time.
We wear it on our wrists.
We carry it in our pockets.
We have it on our walls.
We even have time to go to the mall.
We have time, but we don't have time to spare.
We don't have time to share.
We sometimes don't have time to care.
We have time, but we use words like
"I'll see you later,"
"Call me soon,"
"Let's have lunch,"
"I'll get back in touch real soon."
There are times we do. There are times we don't.
There are times we will. There are times we won't.
So take the time you have to spare.
Make the time for you to care.
Make time; it's always there.

A Wish in a Prayer

If I found a genie in a bottle somewhere on this land,
and I would dig him out with my own two hands,
and if that genie would be so happy I set him free,
he would grant me a wish; he would grant me three.
I would give two wishes away,
but the last wish I would share with you.
I wouldn't wish for fortune or fame;
that's what most people would do.
I would wish that everyone would come to know *Jesus*;
his wishes are blessing, and they always come true.
If you send a wish up in a prayer,
Jesus will send down a blessing to you.
The genie grants you wishes;
he only grants you three.
Jesus has the best blessing;
he can grant you
eternity.

Angels

God sends his angels with a touch of his love,
For he knows we are weak,
so he tells his angels to help us out
to keep us on our feet.
Angels aren't always in your minds,
for your angel could be the person down the street.
For in your moment of need,
God can call them to be the angel that you seek.
And when your angel begins to speak,
you will thank the Lord for the blessing
and his angel that he let you meet.
So, people, please be careful and please be kind
with the words that you speak.
You too may be the next person
that God calls to be an angel and speak.

Beauty Is More Than Skin Deep

Beauty is more than skin deep,
but ugly is to the bone.
Some place beauty on appearance,
but ugly is like a patriot's tattoo,
a skull and two crossed bones.
The beauty of a person will give something away
just because others are in need,
but the ugly of a person will sell it to them,
even if it's
something they don't want or need.
Beauty comes from the heart, and ugly comes from the mind.
But the ugly that comes from a person,
that which was taught to you.
So let not your beauty be the outer appearance of you.
Let your beauty come from your heart,
and a good feeling will come back to you.

Flowers

Some people will never grow, some will never know,
that there are flowers sent from above
to teach you things like how to live and who to love.
Be thankful that you know your flowers,
and they made you the way you came to be,
and they taught you all these things,
and they taught you them for free.

So smell your flowers and touch your flowers' buds.
Share your flowers with the ones you trust.

Share your flowers with the ones you love.
For all flowers will wilt and pass and for everything that's
here on earth, and nothing will forever last.
One day you will be that flower, and then you will see.
Your stems will wilt, and your seeds will fall to the ground
and grow a bunch of new little flowers all in a row.
Then they will pick your flowers
and share them with their families and friends.
You will be so happy in heaven, smiling with a grin.
So with the flowers you have now,
keep them in your heart and never let them go.
And that special someone seeds will restart to grow.
For the flowers that comes from the heart
will reach the heart; I, for one, surely know.
Share all your flower's thoughts and words.
Share all your flower's dreams
and watch your flower's seeds
will restart to grow.

Good Morning

This is a new day,
Blessed and free.
This is but one day,
You let me live to see.
I'll call your name
And give praises to thee.
Thank you, Lord Jesus, for this day
I am so blessed you let me live to see.
Thank you, Lord *Jesus*,
For all the things
You have done for me.
Thank you, thank you, and thank you
Because you've first loved me.

Happy Days Are Here Again

Happy days are here again.
Happy days appear again.
Go out and visit someone sick or shut in.
Pick up the phone
and call a loved one or friend.
And you will see their
happy days will appear again.
You be the one that
makes the happy days
appear again.

I Can Only Imagine

I can only imagine the hurt
and the pain we caused you.
I can only imagine the disappointment and the shame that we
caused you. I can only imagine the day we spit and cursed at you.
I can only imagine the day we crucified you.
I can only imagine all these thing you had to bear.
I can only imagine how much you love us
and how much you care.

Today

Yesterday is over; tomorrow is not here.
Today is for the moments so cherish it.
It can be someone's memories
for years and years to come.

I Wonder

Now that yesterday is over, I sit back and sigh. I
look back to yesterday, and I wonder why.
Have you ever wondered why things do or don't ever happen to
you? And why are these things in life the ones we all go through?
Have you ever wondered why little girls like to comb
their doll babies' hair and why little boys do the
things that they do just because of a dare?
Well, I wonder, and I always will. I'll wonder about
today, tomorrow, if it's the Good Lord's will.
I wonder . . .

A Lie

Never tell a Lie.
They are like potato chips.
You can' t just tell one lie;
you have to tell two or three.

JCU

JCU throughout the day.
JCU Monday through Friday,
Saturday, and Sunday.
JCU when you do good will.
JCU when you are sick or ill.
JCU all day and all night.
JCU when you turn off the light.
JCU twenty-four hours a day.
(*Jesus* sees you always.)

All of Us

Everyone wants to be loved.
No one wants to be disgraced.
Everybody wants to win.
Nobody practiced for second place.
Everyone wants to be happy.
No one wants to be sad.
But tomorrow morning, if you wake,
you should be very, very glad.

Just in Time

A man was walking down the street, and he saw a house on fire.
He ran in and saved a cat.
He got there just in time.
A guy was driving his car so fast that he didn't see the sign.
And when he had to hit his brakes,
He stops just in time.
Today, at work, a lady got up from her desk
To get a drink of water; as she turned and walked away,
A light fixture fell down on her desk.
She walked away just in time.
All these things were just in time, but that's really not true.
Our Lord and Savior stopped by to pay them a visit;
He's always on time.

Listen

Have you ever seen the sun as it peeped
through the clouds but it didn't shine on you?
But as you took a step one way, it shines all over you.
This is God's way of talking to you.
You better take time to listen
to hear what he want to say to you.

Memories

For the memories you have saved,
So deep in you, they are engraved.
In time, those memories may start to fade.
But in you, those memories are still saved.
(Pull up a memory and see.)

Marbles

Why put away all your marbles for a rainy day?
Stop and play with some of your marbles
Because it's raining somewhere every day.

Kick 'Em

Never kick a man when he's down. He might beat you up
when you are on your way
back down.

Math

One plus one plus one equal three.
But in God's eyes, one man, one woman,
and one child equal one family,
not three.

My Father, My Hero

My father, my hero.
My father, my Friend.
My father and his presence made me
his little big man.
Every day I watched my father;
he was always there.
He taught me how to respect my elders;
he taught me when to care.
My mother taught me my ABCs,
but my father taught me how to count my 123s.
My father is my hero,
and he was always there.

Our Holiday

A mother, a father,
a sister or brother,
to them, I take nothing away.
But out of 365 days in a year,
I wish that there would be
one
father and daughter day.

A Delivery Man

I'm your local delivery man.
I deliver flowers by words and not by hands.
For it's the Father that plants the seeds.
And man just watches them grow.
So to the Father, we give him the props
and to the Son that paid for the seeds,
and they are guaranteed to grow.

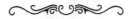

People and Material Things

Some people think that material things
should bring you fortune or fame.
Some people feel that if their house is bigger
and they have a swimming pool, then their kids
should go to the best of schools.
Some people think that if their clothes cost more,
and their car does too, then they should be the boss
to watch over you.
Some people feel that if they make lots of money,
and they can donate what they want to,
then they should have a blessed day and ask what about you?
Well, I don't have a big house with a swimming pool.
My car is old, but it will do. My kids are happy, and they
have lots of friends. And I don't make as much money
as you, but if I see the sun rise tomorrow morning,
then I will have a blessed day, just as you.

People and material things . . .

People

People are different, and this is true.
People are different, just like you and me.
Some people are born small, fat, skinny, or bald.
Some people grow to be cute, handsome, or tall.
Some people are born with a silver spoon,
and I am happy for you.
But some of us are born needing a little help
or handout or two.
Some people will like you for the things you do.
Some will like you for the things you will say.
Some people won't give you the time of day.
There is good and bad in all of us,
so be careful who you love, and be careful who you trust.
So here's something we all can do:
Be quick to listen and slow to say
what we will and will not do
on this wonderful day.
If you should judge someone today, please be careful
for words you say because someone else has already judged you
once or twice today.

Sisters/Sisters-in-Law

For my sisters and sisters-in-law, they're just plenty.
My sisters are special, yes, indeed.
The ones I have, I am well pleased.
To each of my sisters, I look in the face.
I see a different body style, beauty, and grace.
If ever I need my sister, she's always there.
It doesn't matter when, how, or where.
Sometimes, in the game of life, I may slip and lose my sight.
That's when I turn to my sisters for wisdom and for might.
When I go to my sister with tears falling down,
she'll reach out and catch one before it hits the ground.
She'll always hand it back to me and say, "Now be a better man."
And for a few moments, I'll say to myself,
"I think I can, I think I can,
I really think I can." I know a sister everyone needs.
Will I give up one of my sisters? No, not one of these.
To hurt one of my sisters, for that you will regret.
For I'll be the first in battle and on that you can surely bet.
I say to my sisters, with all my heart, until the end of time,
I love you, I love my sisters, in marriage and in birth.

My sisters and sisters-in-law . . .

The World Lives On

The world looks brighter on this day.
The clouds are fluffy and white
and in the sky; there's no sign of gray.
The world looks brighter on this day.
The grass looks green, and the trees are standing tall.
And on the other side of the mountain,
I can see a waterfall.
The world looks brighter on this day.
I can see the ocean and its deep blue sea.
I see many little fish as they swim their lives for free.
The world looks brighter on this day.
Oh, I forgot to tell you
that yesterday (I passed away).
P.S. The grass will grow, the fish will swim,
and birds will fly.
And one day you too will die.
But the world will live on.

Veterans and Retirees Salute

To the veterans and retirees of today,
we salute them because they led the way.
Some of them went off to war as boys,
but they came back as men.
And if our country would ask them,
most would do it again.
Their jobs were just little wheels,
helping the big wheels run.
Every wheel was important until the job was done.

Our troops were out there fighting,
with weapons large and small.
They weren't just for themselves;
they were fighting for us all.
And when the bombs were falling from the air,
sending thunder and lightning everywhere,
some of our troops were crippled, some of them went blind,
some of them lost body parts, some were left behind.
We give our regard to those troops
and to the ones that are gone.
We also give regard to the ones that were wounded,
but they still kept fighting on.
And we will be fighting for peace on earth
and good will toward all men.
So to the veterans and retirees,
of the red, the white, and the blue,
we, the people, in the audience,
the bleachers, and in the pews,
we clap our hands as we salute you.

A Note from Momma

I didn't want another year to pass without giving you my heart felt love expression in this note. I thank God for giving us Children that's loving and caring, especially now that your father and I are in our fall and winter seasons of life. You do so much for us, when I think about it. My eyes water up tears of Joy and Praise. I think about you all having lives of your own, but still you find time for us.

Mom and Dad

Are You a Giver or Taker?

Are you a giver or taker? Do you give more than you take, or do you take all that you can because you say you have nothing else to give?

Are you a giver or taker? Do you always have to win, or do you sometimes slow down and give them a break just so they can cut right in?

Are you a giver or taker? As the conversations begin, do you take over the topic, or do you let someone else get their opinion in?

A giver is a person that lives their life freely. They are not concerned about the fact to be all they can be.

A taker is a person that always has to win. They are not concerned with you; their only concern is I, I, or me.

So take the time to give and give the time it takes. The more you give and the less you take, the better this world will be.

Are you a giver or taker?

Be the first to give.

Fast to Slow

Fast, kind-of-fast, or just plain slow, these are the speeds we as people like to go.

The fast are in a hurry; they are always on the go to the mall or a restaurant or even to a picture show.

Fast, kind-of-fast, or just plain slow.

The kind-of-fast aren't really fast, but they do exceed the speed, sometimes about five or ten miles per hour. The kind-of-fast aren't really fast; they just don't want to be caught going slow.

Fast, kind-of-fast, or just plain slow.

The slow only knows one speed, and that's just plain slow. For they are in no hurry; they have no fast place they want to go. The slow know the faster you go, the more money you blow, and on a cruise ship is where they want their money to go.

Fast, kind-of-fast, or just plain slow.

The next time you pass someone going just plain slow, look back at them in the mirror, and you will see them smiling, for that's more money for them to blow.

Fast, kind-of-fast, or just plain slow.

What is your speed, the speed you like to go.

Would you? I would.

What if you could meet the man that taught Martin, Malcolm, and Mandela to speak wisely? And for $200, he would teach you to speak wisely.

Would you? I would.

What if you could meet the man that taught Michael Jordan, Shaq, and Doctor J to jump high? And for $400, he would teach you to jump high.

Would you? I would.

What if you could meet the world's greatest doctor that could fix broken bones and can make the blind see? And for $600, he would teach you to heal the sick.

Would you? I would.

Well, I know a man that can teach you to speak wisely, he can heal the sick, and he can make you jump with joy. But he doesn't want $200, $400, or $600, and he will teach you all these things for free, if you would.

Believe in your heart and confess with your mouth and through prayer all things can be done.

His name is Jesus.

If I Could Paint

If I could paint, I would paint a pretty picture for your eyes to see. I would paint mountains, valleys, oceans, and seas. I would paint birds flying over tall oak trees as they glide their little bodies through a warm and gentle breeze.

If I could paint, I would paint a sailboat as it glides across the top of the sea, with its sails fully open as it's being pushed around by that warm and gentle breeze.

Well, I am not a painter, so none of these things you will see. The only thing that I can paint is that warm and gentle breeze.

My Father's Son

The man that I became to be, for it was not my will, and you will see. It was the will of my father for his namesake for me to be.

My father's life was built on courage, sacrifices, and demands. It was passed to him that way by his father but with a strong stern hand. He passed it to me that way, so I too will become a man one day.

I have learned from my father for me not to dispute, or I sometimes would get the hand or his big wide boot. I am glad he taught me to walk, talk, and stand. So I'd know how to carry myself as a strong gentleman.

I give thanks to my father for the things he whispered in my ear. I will hide them in my heart, and I will keep them close and dear. He taught me things like always look a man in his eyes, he will respect you more, that's why; a man should work to feed his own; a man should always defend his home; hold your head up high and never quit and never tell a lie.

For my father's name's sake, I will not disgrace. For the love of him that's in my heart, I will keep the faith. So if I should ever have a son one day, I'll teach him this in the same way. So I can sit back and watch him grow and become a man one day.

My father taught me how to seek
these words of wisdom that I speak.
I am the son of a man.

Our Family

To my family, here's a special note. For in my heart is a feeling, and I will hold it close.

Our family is large in numbers, our offspring are too. Every night we go to bed; someone will watch over you.

There are family larger than the one, with me and you. But they don't have a clue on what a family should be like or do. Our men are strong like the might oak tree. Our women are blessed with beauty, just take a look and see. Our children are happy and healthy as can be. Our grandkids are, hum, let's just wait and see.

Our family has lots of loving care. If someone should try to break us up, for them I do dare. Because one of us will stand, than another, than two. And we will fight our hardest for the love of you and me.

We can't tell our future, but we can see our past. I, for one, know our family's love will last.

In our family, our names are different, but we see eye to eye. We will remain a family until the day we die.

Our family is strong.

Seventeen at War

Although, Momma dearest, we have parted, your love, I carry on. Don't worry, Momma dearest, one day I will be back in your arms.

It may be a month or two, or it may be tomorrow, so put a smile on your face to cast away your sorrows.

So, Momma dearest, hold your head up high and say to the service, "My son has gone, but I won't worry about him because he will be coming home."

Yes, I will be coming home one day in the coming year, so let your smile be as the sun and the rain, not be as your tears.

So, "Momma dearest," for as long as you are happy, I will be happy too.

So cheer up, Momma dearest, until my time through.

I do, Momma dearest, I do love and miss you.

What Room Is It?

While in this room, there's a cabinet that has no lock or key. There are things in this cabinet, starting from A to Z. Some of them are old, some of them are new. Some of them you don't remember, but they were prescribed to you.

What room is this?

Have you ever wore your glasses for so long that they felt like part of your face? As you step into the shower, you didn't even notice that you had them on until you went to wash your face.

What room is this?

What's the name of this place? While in this room, we bathe, we cry, we shower, and we shave. We do no. 1. We do no. 2. Heck, I do, and you do too.

What room is this?

B

What Will You Say?

Yesterday I met a man, one whom I thought I didn't know. But he told me the story of how we met over some ten years ago. All I remember was that I gave him a dime, then I turned and slowly walked away. The man said that he used that dime to call his wife, to tell her that he was sorry and that he would make everything okay.

Early this morning, I walked into a restaurant to have a bite to eat. I picked no particular restaurant. I picked no particular seat. As I was placing my order, the waitress said, "Hey, I remember you, you were in here just last week, and you left a tip. Around here, folks seldomly do."

These two stories may have no meaning, at least not to you. But all I am trying to do is to get you to think of how other people view you and what are they saying about you. If you go back to a place that you've visited, once or twice, a week ago, or even sometime last year, watch to see if they approach you smiling as they remember when you were just last there.

Some people will say that they don't care about what others have to say. But they should remember that on Judgment Day, someone will be talking to you about your life, and he won't want to hear what you have to say.

What will you say?

A Greeter

One day I was walking down the street, and I was a little mad because the bus had made me late for a very important date. I walked past the policeman, the mailman, and the store clerk, and to none of them I did speak. I walked by a church, and I saw a little girl sitting on the steps, and we caught eye to eye. She said, "Hello, mister." I quickly lowered my head, and I kept walking by. The little girl said, "Hey, mister, can you hear or speak?"

I looked at her, and I said, "I can hear, and I can speak. I've just had a bad start of this here work week."

The little girl said, "That's no excuse, mister, for you not to speak. If you have a tongue and you can open your mouth, you should be very glad to speak."

So I raised my head, and I said, "Hi," then I lowered my head, and I kept walking by.

Well, I said to myself that little girl sure got me straight, and that was no joke. So after that little girl, to everyone at work I walked by that day, I opened my mouth, and I spoke. The next day I walked down that same street, and I couldn't wait to get to the church, so to the little girl today I would speak. And she was there, and I said, "Hi," and she replied, "Hello, mister," then I smiled, and I kept walking by. She was a pretty little girl; her hair was long and curly, her eyes and skin color were brown, and she was wearing a long pretty white gown. The gown was so long that it laid on the ground, and you couldn't even see her legs or her feet. So for every day for the rest of that week, she and I, we would speak. One day over the weekend, I called to the church to ask what was the little girl's name. They said "Angel" was her name and that she was a special little girl just waiting to be adopted. So I thought to myself that it wouldn't take long, because to everyone that the little girl saw she would speak to or greet. On the first day of the following week, as I was getting ready to go to work, I stubbed my toe on a chair, and it started to hurt. So I called in to work to tell them I was hurt, and today I wouldn't be coming in to work. The next day, as I walked by the church, I didn't see my new little friend. The next two days, again and again, I didn't see my friend. On Friday, I realized that maybe she got adopted and moved away. So I called the church to check and see who the blessed family was that adopted her and to hear how happy the little girl must be. I was told on Monday that *God* adopted her because no one down here wanted to adopt a little girl who has no legs or feet. That is why the little girl wanted to sit on the steps, so to everyone she saw, she would give her very best to speak to or greet. She now lives with God, and she has a loving home. If you should be blessed to make it to the Pearly Gates, and they should open for you, she would be the first angel that would come to greet you and to welcome you to your new heavenly home.

Food

I walked up to the door and opened it, and then I walked in. I heard someone saying grace, so I bowed my head, and in the prayer, I joined in. After the last "Amen," I opened my eyes to see. Right there in front of me was a meal fit for a king. There were tables filled with food as far as I could see. I saw turkey and dressing, ham and chicken, and some collard greens. I saw mashed potatoes and gravy, coleslaw, corn, and peas. I saw some cornbread and a big ole pot of beans. I saw some of my cousins, homemade macaroni, and cheese. And over on another table, it was filled with dessert. There were chocolate cakes, carrots cakes, rum cakes, and a cake made upside down. There were apple pies, cherry pies, and a big ole sweet potato pie. I saw iced tea and punch, coffee, and Kool-Aid, my favorite flavors, grape and red. There was soda pop in one cooler and beer and wine in another cooler, out back behind the shed. Just looking at all that food made my stomach start to grumble. Then suddenly, I woke up, and I realized it was all just a dream. And there I was lying in my bed; I quickly closed my eyes to go back to sleep. I even pulled the covers back up over my head.

All that food . . .

Your Heart and Head

Your heart and head are two different things, but remember there's one body to catch all the love and pain. Your head knows what your eyes see and your heart feels that what your eyes can't see.

Your head may think one way, and your heart may feel the other, trying to use them both together may get things kind of cluttered.

There may be times when your head tells your heart that it's the right thing to do, but your heart said, "No, it's not right for me to do."

Then there are times when your heart and your head get things cloudy and confused. Your heart may tell your head to stay in a relationship, even if you are being hurt or abused.

So here is something we all should do: When others are dealing with you, use your head. But when you have to deal with others, open up and show them your heart instead.

Your heart and head . . .

Mothers

I used to know some mothers, but that was long ago. These are the mothers I write about because these are the mothers I know. For if, as a kid, you said or did something that was not nice or sweet, a real mother wouldn't hesitate to knock you off your feet. It wouldn't matter if your mother wasn't there, for it could be the mother down the street that put you on your seat. Then she would pick you up and walk you home for her and your mother to meet. Those were the mothers I used to know; those were the mothers that watched me live and grow. I remember going over a friend's house after a track meet. As I walked in the door, his mother said to me, "Hello, young man, sit down and pull up a seat. You are just in time, with us, to have a bite to eat."

After the meal was over, his mother brought out a treat. She brought out some peach cobbler; boy it was good and sweet. Those were some cooking mothers, and you could surely tell, the way their kitchens would give off that sweet aroma smell. If one of those mothers should ever say to you to watch what I say, my money's going on that mother; she won't be wrong that day. To mothers of yesterday, I would like to say, please pass on what you've learned to the mothers of today so their kids can say that they have learned from a mother, one from yesterday. So to all mothers, I hope, I wish, and I pray for you to have a wonderful Mother's Day.

Those were the mothers I know.

My Dear Friend

I have a friend that's both young and old. His body has aged, but his heart is as good as gold. He may not be able to do the things that he once did as a kid, but in my lifetime, I wish I could do half the things that he did. He taught me things like gardening and how to watch things grow. He taught me that watermelons grow best on a hill and corn is planted in rows. There are some people that will come in your life, and some will go. So you should be thankful for the ones in your lifetime, you have come to know. So I'll hold on to the memories, and I'll never let them go. I just want to tell my friend that I'll miss him and I want him to know.

P. S. My seventy-seven-year-old friend moved back to the city,
My dear friend Mr. Young . . .

My Biological Clock

Today my car odometer clicked over one hundred thousand miles, and just then my biological clock ticked, and I began to smile. I gave thanks to my car for the many miles together we've went. And to the Father, I gave him his props for my biological clock. Just then three fast cars passed me. Zoom, zoom, zoom, they went. So I wanted to see what my car and I could do. So I waited until they got far up ahead of me. Then I tapped my horn and clicked on my cruise. I planned on being around another lifetime and my car to get another one hundred thousand miles or two.

My biological clock . . .

Funeral

At my funeral, I would like to say a word or two. Some might say I left a note for you. Please listen to what I have to say. Please don't let this day turn you old or gray. Don't cry for me, but I should cry for you. I know how rough life can be for you. For if your eyes could see what I see, all down there would trade places with me because I have a mansion on a street paved with gold. The water here is aqua blue; just to bathe in it will cleanse your soul. I see a line forming just to greet me. I see my mother, father, family, and friends as they all line up to ask me how my life has been. I'll tell them all I lived my life happy and free. And I knew that the Lord was watching over me. For I loved the Lord, my family, and my friends, and if I were down there, I would do it all over again. I knew the Lord told us the things he would do, and he would keep his hands wrapped around me and you. So as I say these words to you on this day, please don't let it turn you old or gray. Search for the Lord each and every day. Look to heaven and always pray. And you will see what I say that there will be a mansion waiting for you one day.

P. S. So let me go. I'll see you soon.
I'll be one in heaven, helping
build your rooms.

Phyllis

As I viewed her body, I see her lying there. I raised my eyes toward heaven, and I begin to stare. I can see her in *God*'s hands, in tender loving care. While on her way to heaven, by grace and by faith, that's right, *God* call an angel messenger, with wings of gold and dressed in pure white. *God* whispered in her ear, for not a soul to hear, "Go tell her loved ones she is getting near."

As that angel opened her wings, there was a certain glow. As she flapped her wings once, she flew straight up in a row. As she flapped her wings twice, she was almost there. As she flapped the third time, there was no room to bare because the angel had already landed on one of heaven's squares. The angel saw a man singing while sitting on a rock. The angel said to the man, "Please don't stop, but I know that you care that one of your loved ones is on her way here."

The man said, "Who? Who can it be? I guess it's like always, we have to wait and see. So I'll go and tell my loved ones, family and friends, that someone special will be coming in."

The man told another; he smiled and grinned. They told Grandma the news that they heard. She told Grandad to hurry, go and spread the word. Grandma told the family, "Don't you dare be late, we will all greet our special loved one at the Pearly Gate."

God placed Phyllis at the golden gate. As she raised her hand to knock, the gates flew open wide. And all of them shouted, some of them even cried, "It's Phyllis! It's Phyllis! Come on in, we are all your loved ones, family and friends. Now that you're here with us, we'll never let you hurt."

As everyone greeted her, her body begins to shake and jerk. At that time and moment, her hands, back, or feet didn't even hurt. She yelled out loud, "God is good! God is good! Let us all be proud."

She looked over yonder and saw the streets paved with gold. She said, "I think I can, I think I can, I'll just run to the end of gold."

She looked back at her loved ones, family and friends, and said, "I'll just run to the end of gold."

They all jumped with joy to see heavenly grace. For this is not like down on earth; this is heaven's place. The street of gold is like eternity, for they will never end. God made Phyllis an angel messenger. She asked the Lord for shoes of gold so she can run from heaven to earth and not leave her footprints or sole. Just then my eyes opened wide from this vison or this dream. And I was standing there, staring up at heaven, with a gleam. All at once it hit me; a smile filled my face, with lots of hope and loving care for the whole human race. For I know that heaven will always be. I hope and I pray to see if the Pearly Gates one day will open up wide for me. So if I should see someone hungry, homeless, or hurt, and someone should ask me, I'll tell them, yes, I care, every time, any place, and everywhere.

My very first vision or poem . . .

My aunt Phyllis passed away with a bad case of rheumatoid arthritis.

Smile

A smile is placed upon your face. It shows your heart filled with loving grace. No one knows why we smile like we do. But it starts with a happy thought and then a chuckle or two.

We smile all the time, and here's just a few:

We smile when we are laughing.

We smile when we play.

We smile when we are happy.

We smile pray.

We even smile when we are hurt, upset, or sad because a smile is just a frown turned upside down.

> So watch what I say and see what you do.
> 1. Start with a happy thought.
> 2. Now make a chuckle or two.
> *See, see,*
> What did you do?

You are the type of person who can smile the whole day through. You are the type of person that can make others smile back at you.

Be the one who smiles first.

Small Towns

Small towns are happy and free; there's no big corporation trying to take over thee. Small towns' stores are owned by a general, some might say. He wasn't in the service, but he's okay. Small town's people drive trucks, and they drive them slow because they are in no hurry; they have no fast place to go. Small town's people sit and rock their time away because on this day, no harm will come their way. Small town's softball games always last past daylight, and their drive-in movies only open on Fridays and Saturday nights. As I look out, I can see fields of corn, beans, and hay as the small town farmers sit back and watch them grow day by day. In small towns, you can see for miles around. There are no tall buildings to look up to, and there's no one throwing trash on the ground. I know that there will always be small towns in the good old USA because people like you and I and what we always say, that when we grow old, in a small town community is where we want to stay.

That Feeling

Is it as that of a mother eagle as she feeds her baby chick? Then all of a sudden, she notices that one of her babies has gotten too big for the nest and after the meal she must give a kick. As the baby eagle tumbles toward the ground, he tumbles over and over and over, spinning upside down. Just then the mother eagle begins to wonder, *Will this be my little eagle's first day of flight, or will this be my baby eagle's last day of life? Will he remember the things that I said, or were they just words that went from ear to ear and then flew straight out of his head?* as that mother eagle watched to see what he would do.

Then suddenly, the baby eagle began to flap his wings, then straight up in the air he flew. He flew high as he soared the sky, never to return to the nest and never to tell his mother goodbye. This is one of those feelings we, as parents, sometimes get, when one of our babies get too big for our nest and we must give them a kick. And we too will watch to see what they will do, if they will soar to the sky or tumble down, crashing their little bodies on the hard and concrete ground. And silently, we will pray that we taught them well. And we'll wish for them the very best. But still, we will get that feeling as we hope that we have no regrets.

The Title of a Man

I grew from an egg in my mother's womb. My mother and father were proud that they gave birth to a new baby boy. From a baby boy, I grew into a kid. I did all thing that the other kids did. Later I grew into a young adult. I learn that if I say "I did it, and I won't do it again," it can help a lot, even if you've just got caught. Quickly, I learned the meaning of phrases like, "yes, ma'am," "no, sir," "thank you," and "please." These can earn you a title of being a young gentleman with ease. Life still had a lot in store for me to become a man, and I would see. When I got a job and I worked hard, I became a hardworking man. Later I became a husband when I took on a wife. She made me a father, with a son and a daughter and their precious lives. First, being an egg, then a baby boy, a kid, a young adult, a gentleman, a hardworking man, a husband, a father, and now some call me grandpa. The kids call me mister. The young adult call me sir. The hardworking men call me a wise old man. Even at the end of life, there are still a few more titles for a man to earn. While written on his headstone, these words should say, "Here lies a *beloved* man and our dear, dear friend."

The title of a man . . .

The Weather

There are more tornados, earthquakes, and hurricanes on a global scale. Man makes more predictions about the weather, but he still can't tell. The weather is one thing that man can't control. Man can't make a twister and tell it which way to go. All these weather conditions are on climate control. God holds the remote, and he is in control. God can make it snow over here and pour out a thunderstorm on you. So you better take heed about the weather. God is getting ready. What about you?

The weather . . .

The World Is a Great Place

The world is a great place and can strive in harmony, only if man let it be. But the man that we know has to be in control. Man now controls the land, the sea, and the air. God created all creation, and he gave each their fair share. Man wants to dominate, to tell the birds where they can fly in the air. But that's just the nature of man, and that's not fair. Man wants to rule over his own brother man. He'll take away his right and freedom; he'll take away his own brother's land. What will this world be like when man is through? Where will man go next? It looks like we're heading to the moon, and it looks like it will be soon. The world is a great place, if man just let it be.

A Play Place for Me to Roam

As a child, I played with balls and rattles, things with mirrors, and car keys. I played on slides, seesaws, monkey bars, and swings. I played on school yards, play grounds, alleys, and hills. I even gotten inside of tires and rolled down hills. I played it cool at the prom and on homecoming night; that was the first time I got everything right. Now, as a parent, with a wife and four kids pulling and tugging all day long, I search and I search for a play place, one for me to roam. All I have found, while in the house, was the TV remote I can control. But out in my garage is my only play place for me to roam.

We've Won

One day, as I was walking into a place of business, a Christian man walked up to me and said, "My brother, how bad can it be? I saw you as you walked in. Your head was down, and your shoulders were slump, and I could tell that Satan was ridding on thee."

Well, I told the man my story; he smiled and grinned. He said, "Satan is trying to steal your joy, but as a Christian man, don't you dare give in. For he is a thief and a liar, and he will steal your joy. Then he will pull the wool over your face so you won't be able to receive the Lord's goodness, mercy, or grace. So tell Satan to get behind thee, for this battle has already been won. For we give God the glory, for this here battle, he has just won."

Just then my shoulders set up straight, and a smile filled my face. For I knew I could take more from Satan because the Lord has just given me more strength and more faith.

This battle we've just won . . .

What Would You Do?

As I sit and think a while, I look and listen, then I begin to smile. Here's something we all can discuss: If you were king, what would you do to us? Would you make us carry you all over town? Would you make us bow down on our hands and knees and face to the ground? These are some things that a king would do. If you were a king, what would you do? What would you do if we polluted your water and air and your birds and your fish started dying everywhere? Would you be mad and treat us rough until we cleaned this mess all up? These are some things that a king would do. What would you do if we cursed and threw rocks at you and we hung you up and stuck a knife in you? Would your call your father and say kill that one and that one too? These are some things that a king would do. We all know that there is a king over all kings too. Let's see what that king would do. If you ask for forgiveness with all your heart, *Jesus* would forgive you . . .

because he cares about you and me.

Who Will Come to Visit Me?

As I lay here in my bed, in my hospital room, I begin to wonder, as I wait to see, who will come to pay their respect? Who will come to visit me? Will it be one, or will it be two or three? For all the good deeds that I have done in my life, who will come to visit me? How about that old lady whose cat I rescued from out of that tree? She gave me hugs and kisses. She thanked me once, then she thanked me again, saying, "Thank you, young man, thank you, you are an angel to me." Will she be there to wish me away, or will she not have the time of day? Will it be one, two, or three? Who will come to pay their respect? Who will come to visit me? How about that man, the one I pushed out of the way of that rolling truck? He was saved by me that day, but I was the one that got hit by that truck. Will he come to pay his respect, or will he even remember that day? That day his life was saved by me. Will he be one, two, or three? Who will come to visit me? Well, I don't know. I'll hold on and wait and see. Who will pay their respect? Who will come to visit me. As I look out my window of my hospital room, I see the sun begin to set and moon begin to glow. The guests begin to say their goodbye, and they begin to go. Who will come to pay their respect? Who will come to visit me? As my eyes get heavy and they started to close, the Lord stopped by to pay me a visit, and he said, "Hi. come live with me."

The Lord stopped by to visit me.

A Friend

A friend is like a brother or sister, which may or may not be kin. This is someone you can tell your secrets to; this is someone you call your friend. A friend will always tell you the truth, even if it hurts them or you. A friend may not always say the words you want to hear, but in their heart, they hold your feelings close to them and dear. A friend will be there when you're on top. That same true friend will be there when you bounce from where you were dropped. Some friends will last a lifetime, and others will carry their weight in gold. A true friend will want to be there when you turn old and gray.

A friend is

Faithful
Reliable
Inspiring
Encouraging
Nice
and Dependable

A friend should be most of these.

He, We, and I

He lived,
　　He taught,
He died,
　He rose,
And he will come again.

We saw him,
　We heard him,
　　We were taught and fed by him,
　　But still, we crucified him.

I heard.
I believed.
I confessed.
I received.

And I one day will go to live with him.

You Too Can Write a Poem

From time to time, things bound around in my head. Then I'll take the time and write them down to read what I've just said. Then I'll close my eyes and say the words that I just read, and then a feeling will start to move around, from my heart back to my head. Then I'll write it down in a poem, just like the ones you've just read. So later on sometime, when things start to bound around in your head, then you can write them down and share with us what is in your heart and what is in your head.

You too can write a poem.

CPSIA information can be obtained
at www.ICGtesting.com
Printed in the USA
LVHW111112240321
682292LV00001B/155

9 781664 154292